A Thief of Strings

A Thief of Strings

DONALD REVELL

Alice James Books

FARMINGTON, MAINE

ACKNOWLEDGMENTS

Many of these poems originally appeared under the auspices of the following publications. I am glad to acknowledge, with thanks, the editors of each: *American Poetry Review, Conjunctions, Court Green, Five Fingers Review, Gutcult, Indiana Review, New American Writing, Octopus, Rain Taxi, Runes, Saranac Review, Slope, Volt,* and *Washington Square.*

© 2007 by Donald Revell

Printed in the United States

10 9 8 7 6 5 4 3 2 1

Alice James Books are published by Alice James Poetry Cooperative, Inc., an affiliate of the University of Maine at Farmington.

ALICE JAMES BOOKS
238 MAIN STREET
FARMINGTON, ME 04938

www.alicejamesbooks.org

LIBRARY OF CONGRESS CATALOGING-IN-PUBLICATION DATA
Revell, Donald
A thief of strings / Donald Revell.
   p.   cm.
ISBN-13: 978-1-882295-61-6
ISBN-10: 1-882295-61-7
I. Title.
PS3568.E793T46 2007
811'.54–dc22   2007001116

Alice James Books gratefully acknowledges support from the University of Maine at Farmington and the National Endowment for the Arts. ❀

COVER ART: John Frederick Peto, *Old Time Letter Rack,* 1894, oil on canvas, 76.52 x 63.5 cm. Courtesy Museum of Fine Arts, Boston. Bequest of Maxim Karolik. Photograph © Museum of Fine Arts, Boston.

for Ben and Lucie

CONTENTS

I

II

III

I

Indeed, what is Nature but change, in all its visible, and still more its invisible processes? Or what is humanity in its faith, love, heroism, poetry, even morals, but emotion?

— WALT WHITMAN

Landscape: A Delirium

From the cabin of things that never change
I see autumn coming from a sunset,
And I can picture myself in a hat,
Stepping into mornings clean with rain.

The sun is real. Where it rises
New wars prepare new trances
And bad bargains.
The enemy is maniacs. And we, Poem, are with the other side,
The savages.
    (Do we keep reading?)

In a children's book,
Jack & Annie free a bear
From the bear pit.
They make a gift of it
To Wm Shakespeare.
In upstate New York,
A Hasidic child is stolen
And killed by a bear.
     (I am reaching for my hat now,
      Almost all the way to China.)

In the cabin of things that never change,
Li Po teases another poet
About suffering and about his enormous old straw hat.

War *on* terror?
War *is* terror...only ask
The Great Wall falling to pieces

Or Li Po. I am in a trance of
Irrational courtesies,
Irrational discourtesies,
And a struggle which, Poem,
You will never know,
For a day's sobriety.

Jack & Annie
And a bear & a baby,
I can picture them
Riding along the Great Wall
On an enormous bicycle.

It's a too-rough lullaby,
A paradise too early.
Swarming with golden bugs
And wishful thinking,
It's a desert at midday
Falling into the sea.

Landscape with Warhol and the Coming of Spring 2003

Andy's war. Even as the blue jays move in Alabama,
In Baghdad
The camera sees a minaret unmoved,
Hour after hour, and the morning star awakens
Dinning birds into the green transmission,
The live feed.

Reading Ovid today on Ovid's birthday, I stopped
At Itys
Hacked to pieces by his mother and poor Philomela,
Cooked and served up hot to the king his father,
And then everybody became a different kind of bird,
It seems, forever.

The minaret has not moved, and now the morning star is changed
To evening star.
In Alabama this year, the vernal equinox
Occurs in the evening. Ovid's birthday winds down.
Darkness all over the planet is a perfect match
For daylight.

Close to midnight, I'm still awake, reading Ovid again,
Watching Andy's war
Out of the corner of my eye. In Baghdad
The morning is a desert pastel with no wind,
And birds are singing even as the blue jays sleep, I guess,
Around my house.

Delirium: A Landscape

The rabbit is not cold, he comes
Directly from the sun
Which is alive although it's resting
On a little table in Amsterdam, green
In the circle of my Christmas lamp.

The sun is hot if you want it to be.

The book is great if you wish it,
Just as the dove beside me,
Shivering in the acacia is not,
This morning of December 22nd,
Cold.

What was eternity when it was a baby?
A tree in Rochester, New York
Decorated for my sole pleasure by a Jew.
Too, it was the sudden knowledge of Benjamin,
My son, being tall as his mother
Seated beside him in the Cool Place Cuba Café.

I was wrong about Amsterdam.
The little table was not a whore.
The hand that reached into the circle of the lamp
Was warm but white as snow.

O Queen of Shepherds,
Bring whiskey to the workmen,
And may their powers be at peace this Christmas
When they drown in the noonday sea.

May the children, old tricks of God's trade,
Become hallucinations and love me.

The rabbit is not cold because the orchard is on fire.

When I was a sunbeam
I landed in a tree.
I could see the president dying.
I could see the wolves come out of his mouth,
And the rabbit was ashes in their mouths,
Howling.
Love is a thing for my sole pleasure and for yours.
I am violets. You are broth.
God walks on earth.

Landscape Near Biloxi, Mississippi

These barrier islands
Are bodies of the outcast
Killed by bridal parties
And shrimp boats in my
Mythology, e.g. Pentheus,
e.g. Actaeon the hunter
Who could not help but see.

Even as a sweet boy in the gunwales,
The god is a destroyer.
Doe-like at the calm, cool waters,
The goddess is a maw.

How beautiful the haze
Unclothing these islands
Offshore by murder.
Who will cover them now?
It was a sweet haze.
It was a bride in anklets.
It was a just cause blanketed by unjust gods.

The Plow That Broke the Plains

FOR PETER GIZZI

These are the lost threads,
Conversations cut in two by teeth
Or by the sword of Alexander—

Cartoons
Cretins
Barrage balloons
A marriage that ought never to have ended
And returns, each autumn,
To the little stream out front in apple clouds.

The soundtrack swells here.
Horses disappear in every direction.

Melville's *Pierre* is a greater something than we know.

Thinking in the World

". . . all the thinking in the world does not bring us to thought;
we must be right by nature, so that good thoughts may come
before us like free children of God, and cry 'Here we are.'"
—GOETHE, Conversations with Eckermann

Eckermann's sparrows and Goethe's larks are the traffic in Laguna.
Waking in the dark,
I hear two songs at the window, smell
Flowers I cannot begin to count
Through the damp-shut door.
Think well of ignorance.
It drives to the ocean, and there it flourishes.
It eats fruit in the tide pools.
The little clothing it owns
Shrinks away to nothing. Here,
Flowers bring their deep intelligence to bear
Against the mind, and mind's grateful.
Those are sparrows and larks at the window.

Storks

Reading,
I find myself
Praying for animals
One hundred years gone
And more sometimes,
And yes, a few men.

In cathedral towns,
Choirs of children
Gather to sing to heal
The white storks ailing in the steeples.

In ancient Rome,
It was illegal to pay one's lawyer.
Cicero, for example. The money
Would corrupt the advocacy.

Singing to the sick birds heals them with a charm.
I mean as in the Old English—*caerm*—
Bells charming over the hayfields,
Finches charming in the trees.

The children's song is human
But unconcerned with the affairs of men.
So do bees love the bird-of-paradise tree
First thing in the morning sunlight
Striking in!

If one of a mated pair of white storks dies
The survivor stays on the nest,
Protecting the young, never leaving,
Not even to feed or to gather.
And so the young birds starve,
Their sharp cries becoming weaker all the time.

They need charming.
The children's choir is their advocate,
As the rising sun is an advocate,
Incorruptible, unconcerned in prayer with prayer
Or with the affairs of men, charming to honeybees
Striking in.

I was reading when my father died
Who could not read.
My wife was asleep,
And the baby slept beside her.
I went outside to see a house nearby,
A small house covered with green vines
Filled with bees.

I prayed and listened.
I prayed and heard
Nothing concerned with men, including my father.
He wanted nothing to do with them either.
He prayed so.
Once he said
My eyes and my sister's eyes were brown like those of deer.

Bartram's Travels

Thus, sweet yellow
Jessamine,
A decent life
In the woods and
The white dust—
Such little hair,
So light a crown—
Saint Joan will be there
When the fire has died
And the river crossing
Is all but behind us.
We shall be young trees again
Driven by dying into late
Summer blossom,
Whiteness coolly clustered
On the scorched branches
That show no signs of burn.

Burned Acreage

White ash softer than water
And, in the morning, cool
As river water, holds fast
To the form of trees. But living trees
Move far away at the speed
Of fire, hot with it. And now comes
A dragonfly with the same news.

Sap & fire, these are true followers.
Shape's a liar.

Here on the hillside
Through the isosceles door
I see a burning shore.
It might be eternity
Or a temporary standstill:
A fireboat come to anchor,
Ashen masts still rocking there.

Jules and Jim

The sky was very near.
                    Carved in stone
The sky was the hieratic face
                    Of Jeanne Moreau,
And the world was no place.

It was where Apollinaire had died.
It was where windmills had done murder,
Where any man
                    Who is a pony only once
                    To only one child
Joined an army,
Bringing death to the horses
                    And to the guitars inside them.

The sky was very near.
I had a lover,
            And thirty years later comes a letter
And a photograph too sad, too vacant to describe,
Although it is smiling.

Today the sky
            In the Mojave Desert is overfull
With sunrise and moonset.
                    The morning star
Recites a poem of Apollinaire's.
                    In a field over there,
A wild pony runs with music wild behind him in a cloud.

Because of a great movie
I have lived this far this long,
My worlds by worlds destroyed,
But never the sky, which is a lover
I can see right through and see
All the boys running to be near her.

O Rare

A skin of a kind . . . is it the sun?
Is that what I have broken now?
God's absolute sovereignty floats like a feather,
No reason to rise, no reason to fall.
Born, we break through it
In graceful ornaments of garlands, gems and hair.

There are questions and wingspans suddenly.
What is water?
The sun's voice as we go,
The vibration of stars along the surface of the world,
And also an insect
Rafting upon curved, small feathers of blue-white sunshine.

Sometimes, before dawn, I fall asleep
In my morning prayers. It's then
I have the best dream ever.
I see an equestrienne
Riding a plough horse the color of milk
Along a dirt path towards a sunny upland.
The rider is Heaven.
Dotting the hillside in flecks and flares
Are bluebirds and redbirds. They seem
Like flowers for a moment, but then they rise into the air,
Taking the hillside with them to the sun.
The birds are Addiction, a skin to break through,
A prayer already prayed and answered in Eden
Where colors abolish distances
And all the morning dreams are true.

I like television. I don't like death.
Einsam. Saying anything at all
Is a war between the grasses,
An encroachment going forward to eternity
In slowest time. *Einsam*: wisdom without thought.
And so God shows Himself as loneliness:
Naked in the straw, naked
On the shameful crossbeam only hours
Since Gesthemane. I cannot help but smile.
Not even the Lord God, it seems,
Would leave, willingly, a garden.

He must be led away, betrayed, already helpless,
His nakedness foreshadowed by a crazy boy,
Or was it an angel, a nameless one,
Streaking through the Gospel of Saint Mark?
And there followed him a certain young man,
having a linen cloth cast about his naked body;
and the young man laid hold on him:
And he left the linen cloth, and fled from them naked.

Manhood is escape, a complex of addictions,
A grass combat against the earth itself.
I've read about a wine made in Italy
Meant to taste like grasses in bright sunlight.
The grass on hillsides is, I think,
As helpless as God, and as addictive. Yesterday
I was drinking in my garden, looking toward the hills.
I saw a white linen floating in the sky.
An angel.

In the middle,
As in the beginning of our lives,
Bright angels resemble themselves.
What help?
How long has it been since I resembled anything?

I am white grass.
The hair over my heart is wings,
Sharp wings, drowned red dragonflies.
Angel is the only word in any language
Singing won't spoil.
They are
Houses rotting in the sun from rain.
Liberty signaling.
Primroses woven into the rosemary
By no hand, filling the entryway,
Closing the only path into the garden.
No. I was happy with the linen. Yesterday,
I was drinking in my garden, looking towards the hills.
I saw a white linen floating in the sky.
It hovered a long time, furling and unfurling,
Leaving no doubt as to the perfection of its whiteness
All its length.
It rose straight up,
Shrinking but somehow getting brighter all the time.
Then, a pinpoint in the blue,
It flashed white fire and was gone.
Some are hearts, some are gardens:
Proud ambitious heaps and nothing else.

God is flat on the ground. I lie beside him.
Together we can hear the tender,
Unvarying trill of sunlight in the dirt.
(If we had drowned, we would hear the same sound
Moving on the water.) Helplessness
Opens a gate in the dear earth,
Into Eden, Eden everywhere.
Each color is ten thousand hues of itself.

Do you remember Zeno's Paradox?
All it explains is the mating of dragonflies.
There is a dragonfly aimed at my heart.
God too.
What you call dreaming, we
Call the breastbone of an angel
Divided by two.

In the valley of the Little Colorado,
All the morning dreams are true.
In the valley of the Little Colorado,
Where I'd been thrown onto a heap of stones,
Ten thousand hues in the wings of just one insect
Burst from me, and I was high up,
Falling. Birds in the invisible trees
Called to me. They came and clad me for death
In graceful ornaments of garlands, gems and hair.
In the valley of the Little Colorado,
Nearer than you suppose,
A skin of a kind and then the skins of every kind
Broke. The sun was born where it is buried,
Here in my bosom and at home.

A Prism That Is

A leaf, a secret innocence as happens
Inside the leaf, dividing the light
When each color in unity deepens
Imago, a good death;

A secret
Running the length of alleyways in Denver,
Color of cottonwoods when thunder
Steels the sky;

God's lathe;

A hummingbird turning a lathe to make its nest,
And the wind powerless against it,
Going through;

Afterwards,
Imago just one hour,
Sun goes down,
A prism that is
Cool as a leaf, cool
And vaporous as grass
When grass goes home.

II

14 FOR ROBERT CREELEY

Just in the Morning

IN MEMORY OF ROBERT CREELEY, 1926–2005

There are no clouds.
Pink or purple, in a terrible wind,
The locust flowers, having their own minds,
Hang on. Sun's bright, March 30th,
Cloudless sky.
But the ground dark somehow, as though clouds were passing.
Absent or present, death slips beneath.

And above us?
Who's to say there is no one
Already building a fire in the cabin
I see from here, tilted awkwardly
On the mountaintop beside one tree?
The wind seems not to reach that high.
Smoke from the chimney goes straight up.

Good Friday

The clown is hurt between two trees.
His circus went far away, and they are happy there
With many animals, living by the sea.

Here, the low bushes are like little pigs,
And the flowers fierce, with great teeth in them.
I see no animals in the sky, but my mother does.

I see lights under the ground at night.
I hear them digging sometimes, and I know
One morning very early when the house is sleeping,

Creatures no one has ever seen here
Will come up through the floors.
Their faces will be fires. Their fur will smell of earth

And of secret white things, buried a long time.
If I go with them, I will never die.

On My Fiftieth Birthday

How old is when old is
A garden
Or the noise of reproach?
Here as I am
I find myself praying,
Yes, for bees one hundred years dead
And a few men.

It is not ridiculous. The bees
Strike into the sunlight,
Giving it a sound.
The echo is flowers.
One hundred years ago,
And the day has never yet ended,
A few men are praying.

Poplars

The heat blew through my spine into my heart.
My back was to it, the sun.
I crouched, and pain came.
I stood, and there was none.

The wind is a dozen things.
Across my road, where the abandoned cars
Make a mansion-heap, poplars
Mimic tentacles, exactly 12, in the dusty air.

My desert is just beginning.
A little while from now, I will abandon my body,
And a few years after that, the Chinese

Will abandon Peking because of dust storms
Oranging their skies, choking their athletes.
God is the sun truly, you know, and He moves fast.

Icarus

I cannot count the strange animals
Falling through my eyes.
One is not one.

A different one,
Just this morning at sunrise,
Had escaped.
He wore the bright orange of a convict still.

In no real hurry,
He walked away from the sun
Into the mountains,
Orion's rock face.

His back was on fire,
And when the fire became wings
He flew.

Hallowe'en, Blue Diamond, Nevada

These are stars
Made wholly of woodsmoke.
I am drinking to them
As up ahead of me our children
(Three of them: Death,
A Fairy, and tow-headed Starvation)
Go from door to door to get their candy.

I am drinking under a mask,
And the whiskey mixes with the wood-smoke
Kindling stars above me.
I know I feel
The Republic is dying
Because the Republic is dying.
Sweet Jesus gives me candy I can breathe.

Election Year

A jet of mere phantom
Is a brook, as the land around
Turns rocky and hollow.
Those airplane sounds
Are the drowning of bicyclists.
Leaping, a bridesmaid leaps.
You asked for my autobiography.
Imagine the greeny clicking sound
Of hummingbirds in a dry wood,
And there you'd have it. Other birds
Pour over the walls now.
I'd never suspected: every day,
Although the nation is done for,
I find new flowers.

San Clemente

Bird alights, bee alights, child shouts
"For a limited time, free water!"
My dear neighbor's arm is talking in the dirt.
He's building something: houses for turtles.

So early,
The sun shines at ground level, and all trees
Are lit from beneath. To Larry Eigner,
If he were alive, I'd say
Americans aren't taller anymore
Than the cars they drive.

And he would say in reply, or Christ would say,
Never you worry. Late as it is,
Early this morning a bread truck climbed a hill
In southern California, and you saw it.

Moab

Where the later kids grow tall
The talk is colors.
Avert your eyes, nary a vowel,
Avert your eyes.
Dying, like dirt reading a magazine, neither laughs nor cries.

I heard a hissing in the sun at sunrise.
Oh my Savior, this very morning
You must step out of the sun,
Colored in no color at all
But in the sound of grass stains

Waking the snowfields,
Waking even the crags and caverns
Whose simple pleasures are my destruction,
Against whose arrows my sons have nothing to oppose.

Carcassonne

After the ruins,
The cold winds
Came from the south,
And the sun,
Clinging
To the north slopes
Like a greatness wounded,
Withdrew,
Vine by vine by hawk's wing,
Over the last village.
One bell was a fountain.
One airplane made a hole in the sky.
That night starlight
Passed through walls.

"There might be beauty"

There might be beauty.
The wind outside may be
A face really quite plain,
But as a daisy 10,000 miles away,
A stirring, the beginning
Of a beginning to end the world,
And a free hand for innocence.

I have a friend translating Rimbaud.
What's it to you?
To me, he is the horizon of a horizon.
Small creatures conspire and smile
Into the rainbow he is building
For them alone. There might be beauty.
To me, it feels like 10,000 miles of daisies.

Sibylline

My trees are gone yellow to the East.

That's wrong.
That's the afterlife,
Or Argicida at least.

And late at night in the deep chair
When the movie is black & white,
It finds one Deborah Kerr
In tears on the beach in furs,
Connecticut, not Elysium,
And the moon rising from an ocean made of paper.

Why this wild longing
For the world of light?
It's wrong.
It's killing my trees.

After Williams

What is a good place
Sparkling rose-yellow
Mexican lunch wagon broken down
On Rainbow Blvd
Or even closer to home
I wake up
And in the garden Claudia
Is washing the remains
Of a dead sparrow
Out of the fallen garden umbrella
What is a good place
To break down to die
To ask such a question
Is one heaven

What if Christ Were a Snowflake Falling into the Sea?

The water is taller than itself,
Covering spirits of the air beneath.
And so the land, so mountainous beside,
Does not exist.

Have you thought about the future?
Take your finger and rub it across a stone.
Do you feel it?
Heat where nothing but cold most certainly is.

The water does not suspect.
A distant star is plotting with the center of the Earth
Against the Earth.
And the lake rises. The outlet rivers rise.

There is also an uprising in Kiev.
God is love.

III

This is where my love, somehow, stops.
—JACK SPICER

To the Christians

I was one of a pod of dolphins
Living in the sky.
Mycenae. Glad to meet you.

We were not otherworldly,
No more than is a robin's nest
In the scrawny pines.
Babies open bright throats to the sun,
And out of the sun comes food.
It never fails.

Smile for me, Immortality.
You are a certainty.
Otherwise, there is no sky
And no explaining the life in it,
The lilac colors swimming there.

Mycenae. The robins sleep.
Sunshine warms their bellies until morning.

To the Jews

I am the grass I dreamed I was.
Atalanta,
From inside a drop of dew
Comes the speed to outspeed you.
I have seen it.
Imagine something like a cloud, but like diamonds too.

The human eye began as grass.
In the first mornings,
Water raced out of the air
Becoming Soul, who is the speed of things.
I lay my head onto the ground.
Is my dog a god because he kills a rabbit?

I lay my head beside the broken animal.
Our eyes meet. The world belongs to him.

To the Muslims

With four years still to live,
My black dog leapt into the whitewater
At Indian Springs. He was overjoyed,
And joyfully he swam very hard
Against the current, back to me.

I hear what a pagan would have made:
The higher sound is bees;
The lower, a dove alone
Alighting onto a rooftop corner.
All together it is whitewater.

All together it is one God, who never made a desert
And whose circus we are, all clowns swimming.

My dog was not afraid.
He lived four years more.

To the World

You are the last guitar,
A morning of age that ends
In tender, first, and simple noises.

To the north of here, an old man is dying.
To the east, his sister bleeds into her brain.
So it goes. And sometimes it goes very far,
But never close to you, never
In sight of the first mountain
From which I threw myself into the trees
Whose tops are oceans and whose wood,
If I lived, awakened as guitars.

I can't complain. When I am born again, I will begin.
Good world, you are the rumor I believe
When no one's there but me.

The Last Guitar

Le printemps, c'est l'automne,
    the last guitar alive;
De l'aube claire,
    the last guitar alive.

Or is it the golden dog
I always see at home
Running against the sky?
We call him *Roof Dog.*
I cannot imagine my life
If I had never seen him.
I'd know no peace.

Which foreign movies do you like?
All of them.
Coming out of the fog—dogs and words.
And the magic is—they never die,
Not so long as one guitar's alive.

Between French and death
The houses sail like baseballs.
Come into the kitchens . . .
The meals are finished.
All the dishes talk a nonsense on the shining boards.
It is October.
This is the World Series.
We sail on baseballs made of gold.

A house will starve a Jew.
A house will starve a Muslim.
Every house he ever entered
Starved Jesus to death,
And he was the last Christian.

But the world,
Thank God for the world,
It starves the houses.
A golden dog
Leaps across the sagging rooftops,
Baying the moon.
All's well.

I.

I am thinking all the time about serenity, and what it might mean.
I think it means the end of humanity:
When humans wither from the lakes;
When death's granary is full,
And a fading rose weaves the garland of its death;
When, gorged on honey and manna,
Words make moan.
De l'aube claire until the end of days,
The latest dream I ever hope to dream
Will not be human.
What is the meaning of guitar?
Guitar means gloom.

In the royal palm, twilight changes dove wing to bat wing.
Butterfly's unharmful terror stirs fires.
No more to be a man is a change not changing.
If I can think it, it can't be far.

2.

More and still more, *saison brumeuse*, it comes to me
Only this afternoon and very clearly:
For my part, life on earth is only
Possible anymore as snow, as something very close
To melting all its life, as in a city
The snow is a guitar to children waking,
And to women and men a white dove disappearing
Out of the picture frame, autumn of one last love
And never another, close bosom-friend of death.

Now the sun has died, and all the guitars, having melted
Out of the children's hands, become black ice.
Last oozings, hour by hour, freeze beneath the keels of paper
    boats.
The wind dies.
Cybele will not return. *Saison brumeuse*,
In a wailful choir . . . *saison brumeuse* among the sallows and the
    old lambs,
I hear a sinking as of houses and garlands into holes.
Cybele will not return.
If there is no solution,
Can it be a problem?
So much for the sex changes.
So much for the absolute end of humanity.

A boy not human at all wakes in a small room.
His name is Attis and his retinue will be lions.
Thank God for the world and for the snow I became there.
They won't kill me.

3.

As it turns out, eternity
Was a half-reaped furrow sound asleep.
Even dead, the sun keeps shining.
The snow melts, and it is still snow,
Speeding out of the last children's hands
Into the shape of lions. Happy snow.
Happy Attis who has never known
One instance of humanity. He is a warm boy.
He covers himself with bees,
And it is summertime inside him.
The heat spills over into floods.

Knowledge was sad.
Black birds shat onto white birds.
We called it springtime.
White birds ate the shit, and it was fall.
No wonder I've forgotten my schools.
I remember summers and baseballs. Memory
Rides in paper boats on mysteries
Too fast to freeze. *Le printemps, c'est l'automne,*
And so's your old man.
The climate, thinking with its knees,
Knows nothing, thank God.
The last guitar is but the first of many.

Magi

Houses are impossible anymore.
There is a shout in the Christmas trees,
And he is a strong man.

In the cold street,
A discarded chair faces the Sachem Apartments,
And it begins to be a book—

Orphaned by Indians,
Boyhood buddies meet again
When they are strong men,
& the writing desks shatter at their touch,
& rocking horses float on frozen air, hunting,
& Christ is a stronger man shouting in the trees.

The year 2005.
All the orphans have refused our houses.
I see them in the street
In the broken chairs at broken desks.
The splintered wood speaks to them.
It soothes them, I can see that.
And as it happens,
I do not wish to see anything else anymore.

The Birth of Venus

So vines from my fingers
And bees weighted in the vine-shoots
Purring
Sleepily pale clear
My real imaginary girlfriend
1971
I am reading *The Song of Roland*
Speaking for days to no one—
Set the goddess there

And in the Grange Hall
Dreams of havoc
Imaginary Catskills and sparrows
I went in I mean I went in*side* the mountains
Gods to the left
The low
The lion
The grasshopper curved green-gray
And there were no gates anymore

The Wisdoms

It was now late; Goethe gave me his dear hand, and I departed.
—JOHANN PETER ECKERMANN

What happened? I was one
Gladly suffered the believing I am I.
A cut tree weeps a stream of ants from its wounds.
Not two feet away, sage and verbena thrive
In a cascade of blue differences
Over the lizards and dirt.
La di da. To matter to me,
Time was, a man or woman had to love me.
That was America.
That was a chief concern.
What happened is my eyes have no color.
I love the way a flower steps away
From a dead tree.
Broken glass is alive too,
In the colors. In them, I was a republic.

Stoic

My soul is a mind and a meander, a Mrs. Luxe.
Little Spartan boy, release the animal in your shirt!
It isn't a wolf cub, it's a puppy, soon
To be Lassie, and she's needed
For the invasion of Norway, that disastrous offensive.

Her parachute opens.
A minute or so later,
Her paws touch delicately down
Onto the glacier, and instantly
The ice turns a radiant deep sky-blue
Wherever she goes. Peter Lawford
Is rescued and returns to England.
Lassie remains behind,
Changing every inch of the arctic earth into blue sky
Which is becoming my mind.

My soul has turned from now to then.
It's all a luxury, this being alive.
Read me that woman's poetry, I'm watching *King Kong*.
There's an animal up my sleeve, and it's killing me.

Solstice

FOR APRIL & FOR AIMEE

Golden grass in the ice is given music.
It breathes,
And we stand upon its breath,
The last
Rainbow in the state of Maine until Easter.

Can there be any life but this?
Grass freezes
In standing water first week of December.
Ice
Presses the air out of each blade, making
It golden,
Making at just that moment a sound
Of sighing
Strong enough to walk on straight through Maine.

One Christmastime,
Barbara Stanwyck abandoned a station wagon over there.
Years later,
John Ashbery, gentle Pierre Martory and we
Found it
Filled with frozen water filled with gold-green grass.
It was
The soul of God's own movie palace,
Now showing
The state of Maine as breathed in given music
One December,
Which is another life than this.

Thief of Strings

I.

No, different than that, not
Forgotten, gone. The air
In the sky here is sassafras
Wound in shoals, not gone,
Crowded. But the air is alone.
My life's gone out of mind.
Let us see, Sky, but not me.
I'm no company anymore.

The poor thief running out of the guitar shop
Was stopped and searched and humiliated
Not ten feet away from me as I waited
For the train. Down on his knees he gave up
A pocketful of strings, and I couldn't see any more
When the train came. I was safe on board.

Gone. Whatever I'd thought to do was gone
When the doors opened. Must one
Become stupid to ride on trains?
My whole life, from the end of childhood
To this very moment of the sassafras
Wound in shoals, had disappeared.
When I left the train I could hear
Dozens of birds shrieking in the trees.
Let us see, Sky, but not me. I was a child
Once, but that's not me. The birds shriek.
The thief surrendered his pocketful of strings
And my life disappeared. I was a happy child
And nothing since. Cool air. Crimson air.
All along a line of trees I go, coming from nowhere.

2.

Certainly,
There will be singing later,
There will be songs in the car,
And later still, a drive to where the woods are burning.

Early, I was windows and oranges,
Boys with white hair cut straight across their brows,
Girls in white blouses.
Death is a girl in a white blouse, I'm telling you.
Almighty
Everlasting God, now you tell me exactly

Where I have been this long, long time,
And what crime is a pocketful of strings.

I have a paperback with me,
Rimbaud's *A Season in Hell.*
On the cover, a man
Presses his entire body against a windowpane.
What crime?

Happiness and despair are one mind
Of perfect emptiness under unbearable pressures.
(Much later, my son is in the hotel parking lot
Waiting to catch a ball I've thrown too high into the air. It's
unbearable.)
A mind I must never speak, nor you, God.
Better to keep walking down the hotel corridor behind a dog.
Better to steal guitar strings.

3.

ELEGY FOR THE WORD DUSK

Beautiful girl in a flowered skirt on the train,
She heard me talking to myself.
Did I want something?
No, I was only reading aloud
A sign I'd seen—
EDEN CEMETERY
Hours 10 AM Until Dusk.

Has anyone on the train
Spoken this word *dusk* aloud
In a long time?

All along a line of trees I go, coming from nowhere.

Take it for now, a skirt
Is a border of flowers
Surrounding a flowerbed, *ha!*
And it is the sharp edge of the train steps
And the branch that whips across my eye
When I've left the train and am walking
All along a line of trees and beyond them
I see bright windows, the ballet class,
And one of the men presses his entire body
Against the glass.

"I want to go to the Garden of Eden to die."
I seem to have written this down some time ago
In my copy of Rimbaud. It says in handwriting
"Dylan Thomas." I remember poetry just fine,
But nothing of me, not from childhood until the train.

When I was a boy, my father drove us once
Very fast along a road deep in a woodland.
The leaves on the trees turned into mirrors
Signaling with bright lights frantically.
They said it was the end of the world and to go faster.

And now it is dusk.
The air in the sky is sassafras.
I've forgotten to tell you:
Back on the train, an old woman's face
Floated in the reflection of white flowers
Someone held on his lap across the aisle
Bringing to Eden.

4.

SIX GUITAR STRINGS

Evergreen
Burr-marigold
Gentleman
Dogwood
Anybody
Erelong

There was a gentleman in Paradise once a long time ago, and he punished the dogwood, and to the evergreen he granted life everlasting. As for ourselves, we are marigolds, given to thieving.

I mean, if I have forgotten my life, I must steal a life, if only from myself.
(Much later, my son is smiling, having caught the ball I'd thrown.
(And later still, when the woods are burning, he smiles again.

Enjoyment of the world is never right
(You can say that again Traherne, never right unless the wine cups are drained to the lees and filled with sunlight first thing in the morning.)
Till evry Morning you awake in Heaven.
But there comes a time when you've forgotten your life, and all you ever do is awaken, and then it's *Heaven, Heaven, Heaven,* the burden of flowers all the time, and flowers are given to thieving.

I want to go to the Garden of Eden to die.
Happiness and despair are one mind,
And the Devil is another evergreen burr-marigold gentleman.

Dogwood anybody erelong.

5.

SETTING WOODS ON FIRE
(AFTER RIMBAUD)

Much later still
A match I had forgotten
Far from the woods
In a sunny recess
In a hillside
Kindles fire to fight
With boards from a boat
And then with hands and feet.

Father, where will this end?

It will go to town
Daffy and Dilly
Where the air shows through
Showing the folks a new dance.
Clap your hands.

It will be a glorious spectacle, and I will be the only one there to
enjoy it. No stems, no roots anymore, a glorious spectacle, and the
meadows so many mirrors signaling with bright lights frantically. It
never has been done.

Eyelids
Blackbirds
Grosbeaks
Dogfooted
Almshouse
Everywhere

6.

THOUGHTS THAT BLOT OUT THE EARTH ARE BEST.
I COME FROM THE FUNERAL OF MANKIND.

Behind clouds
Orion himself
Begins to fade.
Be brave, child.
Have you seen
With a full moon,
Clouds or no,
Eyes shut tight
Or wide open,
The night is wonderfully bright?

The stars are alone,
Only racing through
The accident of constellations.
Be brave.
You have no mother.
You have no father.
You are a mountain lion
Inside of a star,
The last lion,
And wonderfully bright tonight.

Earth-song something Chinamen go round.
Battlefield.
Goldfinch without fir-balsam, gunmen.
Dog-days.
Ash-colored any day weather cannot damn you,
Everlasting moonlight.

The branch that whips across my eye
Is the child that was I, denying me,
Dazzlingly bright tonight.

7.

The sky is sassafras
And also a balloon landing.
Spring arrives,
Memory's panoply
When it should happen
As it has happened
As sassafras now
And a vase of yellow roses
Dying on a windowsill
There through those trees.

I planned to say,
But there is no plan,
Or rather, not a memory
Of one in this panoply.
The balloon is thousands of flowers
And fragrances, stupid
Only to me and to the poem.
And to the poem I say
I will stay here
Just as long as *flower*
Rhymes with *star*,
And *fragrance* with *star*,
Because a man without a memory
Understands the stars.
He can smell them.
He can hear the winds between them
Whispering futurity on emptiness.

Else-whither
Broom-making
Ghost-like
Dark-violet
Afternoon
Everywhere

But only until the stars come out, the flowers no man with a memory can see.

Else-whither THIEF OF STRINGS *Everywhere*

8.

Shreaming (Ovid) the word in Golding's translation is *Shreaming*
Heavenly word, and my age is now my mother's age when human
   beings
First walked the moon.

What use
Is memory
When any
Instance is
Too many?

I am the boy my father drove
Golding's *Metamorphoses*
Red guitar and black cello
I am the boy my father drove
Shreaming to the moon.

And there were human beings there, ever so few and still too many,
Same as the concert hall
Where just a handful
Is too many to hear,
And so I lay me down
Inside a guitar
Or the cello's scrollwork
When I am the boy my father drove to music in the moon.

Da da DA da DA da da DA da DA

And how the moon turned into Heaven
Is a very good story (Ovid) I've forgotten.

Easternmost archangel, I am the boy my father drove to you.

9.

LADIES and Gentle-MAIN,
With your kind
AttENtion,
and
Permission,

DA da DA da DA
DA da DA da DA

Introducing:
Mr. Memory

Just think of the strain involved by his prodigious feats,
Answering fully and freely
In Alfred Hitchcock's *The* 39 *Steps* . . .

It killed him. "Am I right, sir?"

Why did I not use my eyes when I stood on Pisgah?
Use & commit to life what I can't commit to memory?
Easternmost archangel, now the crescent of the moon is seen
And her attendant star is farther than last night,
And the source of the Nile is a mountain on the moon.

I am not on a train.
I am out of the world
Where the children must go far to school,
The still stagnant
Heart-eating life everlasting and gone to seed
Eden.

Is it killing me?

"They showed me Johnny Ruyaden today—with one thickness of
ragged cloth over his little shirt for all this cold weather—with shoes
with large holes in the toes. This little mass of humanity—this tender

gobbet for the fates, cast into a cold world with a torn lichen leaf
wrapped about him . . .

(I hear just now of terribly burned children in Korea stitched together
with twine.)

. . . O I should rather hear that America's first born were all slain
than that his little fingers and toes should feel cold while I am warm
. . ."

I am not on a train.
I am in Eden
Without a river to my name,
All rivers having gone to the moon.

Easternmost archangel, untune my words and teach me tanager.
Brook-side puppy it was a cuckoo.
Ghost-like commotion it was a Christian.
Dream that we have hundreds of pears, because pears are Heaven
And apples only this life on
Earth.

And so I put this life into a basket and hand it off to Johnny Ruyaden.
This is the use of memory: children stitched together with twine.

10.

Eglantine:
Eyes are pools and the sun a pebble tossed.

Briar-rose:
No rose is sure.

Goldenrod:
My old mind, memory, is a trellis like death.

Daisy:
There were dirty plates on a white day in a black river.

Azalea:
When I was a boy my mother loved azaleas, and they rose from the
    soot to meet her.

Eglantine:
Eyes are pools and the sun a pebble God has tossed.

While all the while
In the interstices and crackling
Of thorns of a trellis, honeysuckle,
Indistinguishable from the death it climbs, climbs and sidles,
And as Alice (Notley) said to me
You cannot kill honeysuckle, i.e.
You cannot kill death, it is born from us,
Born again too, as Jesus saved my death from dying.
What did John Donne know?
It is the rightful pride of death
To raise a wall of flowers where it destroys a wall.

All along a line through my old mind:
Honeysuckle

II.

I found my name on a tree
Reminding me
Of the prows of vessels.
Often as now
Like flames,
Or more like the surf
Curling before it breaks,
The air curls in front of me,
Breaking not into pieces,
But into passages
Leading to flowers
Or to a bird in a tree.
What use to a man
To take his model from a man?
Small as a pea,
The hummingbird's brain
Remembers music more intricate than English,
And makes the music.
What do I remember?
What have I made?
Or God, who in the English of His own
Is a mustard seed?

What use to a man is Man?
We cannot even hear the hummingbirds.
We steal guitar strings.

Expected babe, ghosts dissipate, airy-eyed.

12.

Eager,
So busy, rightly so,
With being so pretty—
Meaning *Tucson*, meaning *friends*—
The little girl bends towards the airplane.
Then she flies
With all the white gladness of an acolyte.

In the desert, birdsong sounds without an echo,
The equal of sunlight.
The bird is one alone.
The sun is one alone,
And, like the dead, alone travels fast and true.
No shoes, no echoes.

So much poetry all over the place about woodland birds,
Their songs echoic—
Many, many, many—
Sounding a depth that isn't true.
Echoes, but still no shoes.

In "nature" there's no choice—
Denise Levertov

Denise, this once I disagree.
The choice a flower makes to catch my eye,
Risking everything;
The hummingbird choosing to alight
Upon this impossibly slender branch,
Not a branch at all, really,
More like a needle;
And she alights, and she is all alone,
Upheld in desert sunlight, singing
Something beautiful I cannot hear
Because it goes so fast
And straight into the sun;
These are choices without the aid of memory.
They are free, not stolen like strings or like shoes from a powerline.

When I was a child,
There was a lady all alone in a cage with nickels.
I gave her my money, and she gave me
A hundred little doors with food behind them.
This one time, I disagree.
Choice is our natures, loosed from memory.
The flower
Is never blinded by the sun it faces freely.
The bird won't fall.
My money was good because I did not make it.
I gave it to the lady in the cage to change.

13.

Outside his shop
In the leafy sunlight
The clockmaker smokes at ease,
Singing a little,
Rapping a cadence
Against his artificial leg
With his good leg.
His shop sign is a broken clock face
Filled with leaves.
These metaphors mix themselves,
And I say hurray for helplessness!

Who made my eyes? Not I.
And an almshouse everywhere?

When I am alone the air
Is flecked with sassafras.
Crowded before me in shoals
Happy shrieks grow old.
I say hurray for helplessness!
What use to a man is Man?

When I left the train I could hear
Singing in the trees. It was the trees
Who sang. When I was a boy
It was the trees who sang. My whole life
From the end of childhood
Until this very moment
Is one bird nowhere.
Not forgotten. Free.

RECENT TITLES FROM ALICE JAMES BOOKS

Take What You Want, Henrietta Goodman
The Glass Age, Cole Swensen
The Case Against Happiness, Jean-Paul Pecqueur
Ruin, Cynthia Cruz
Forth A Raven, Christina Davis
The Pitch, Tom Thompson
Landscapes I & II, Lesle Lewis
Here, Bullet, Brian Turner
The Far Mosque, Kazim Ali
Gloryland, Anne Marie Macari
Polar, Dobby Gibson
Pennyweight Windows: New & Selected Poems, Donald Revell
Matadora, Sarah Gambito
In the Ghost-House Acquainted, Kevin Goodan
The Devotion Field, Claudia Keelan
Into Perfect Spheres Such Holes Are Pierced, Catherine Barnett
Goest, Cole Swensen
Night of a Thousand Blossoms, Frank X. Gaspar
Mister Goodbye Easter Island, Jon Woodward
The Devil's Garden, Adrian Matejka
The Wind, Master Cherry, the Wind, Larissa Szporluk
North True South Bright, Dan Beachy-Quick
My Mojave, Donald Revell
Granted, Mary Szybist
Sails the Wind Left Behind, Alessandra Lynch
Sea Gate, Jocelyn Emerson
An Ordinary Day, Xue Di
The Captain Lands in Paradise, Sarah Manguso
Ladder Music, Ellen Doré Watson
Self and Simulacra, Liz Waldner
Live Feed, Tom Thompson
Pity the Bathtub Its Forced Embrace of the Human Form,
   Matthea Harvey
The Arrival of the Future, B.H. Fairchild
The Art of the Lathe, B.H. Fairchild

ALICE JAMES BOOKS has been publishing exclusively poetry since 1973. One of the few presses in the country that is run collectively, the cooperative selects manuscripts for publication through both regional and national annual competitions. New regional authors become active members of the cooperative, participating in the editorial decisions of the press. The press, which historically has placed an emphasis on publishing women poets, was named for Alice James, sister of William and Henry, whose fine journal and gift for writing went unrecognized within her lifetime.

TYPESET AND DESIGNED BY MIKE BURTON

PRINTED BY THOMSON-SHORE
ON 50% POSTCONSUMER RECYCLED PAPER
PROCESSED CHLORINE-FREE